AF576730

The
New Wave
Pop Music of the Early '80s

by Tim Frew

A FRIEDMAN/FAIRFAX BOOK

Library of Congress Cataloging-in-Publication available upon request.

ISBN 1-56799-498-9

THE LIFE, TIMES & MUSIC SERIES: THE NEW WAVE
was prepared and produced by the
Michael Friedman Publishing Group, Inc
15 West 26th Street
New York, New York 10010

Project Editor: Francine Hornberger
Consulting Editor: Maria Tahim
Art Director: Jeff Batzli
Designer: Robbi Firestone
Photography Editor: Karen Barr
Production Manager: Jeanne Hutter

Grateful acknowledgment is given to authors, publishers, and photographers for permission to reprint material. Every effort has been made to determine copyright owners of photographs and illustrations. In the case of any omissions, the publishers will be pleased to make suitable acknowledgments in future editions.

Color separations by HK Scanner Arts Int'l Ltd.
Printed in Hong Kong by Midas Printing Limited

1 3 5 7 9 10 8 6 4 2

For bulk purchases and special sales, please contact:
Friedman/Fairfax Publishers
15 West 26th Street
New York, NY 10010
(212) 685–6610 FAX (212) 685–1307

Visit our website:
http://www.metrobooks.com

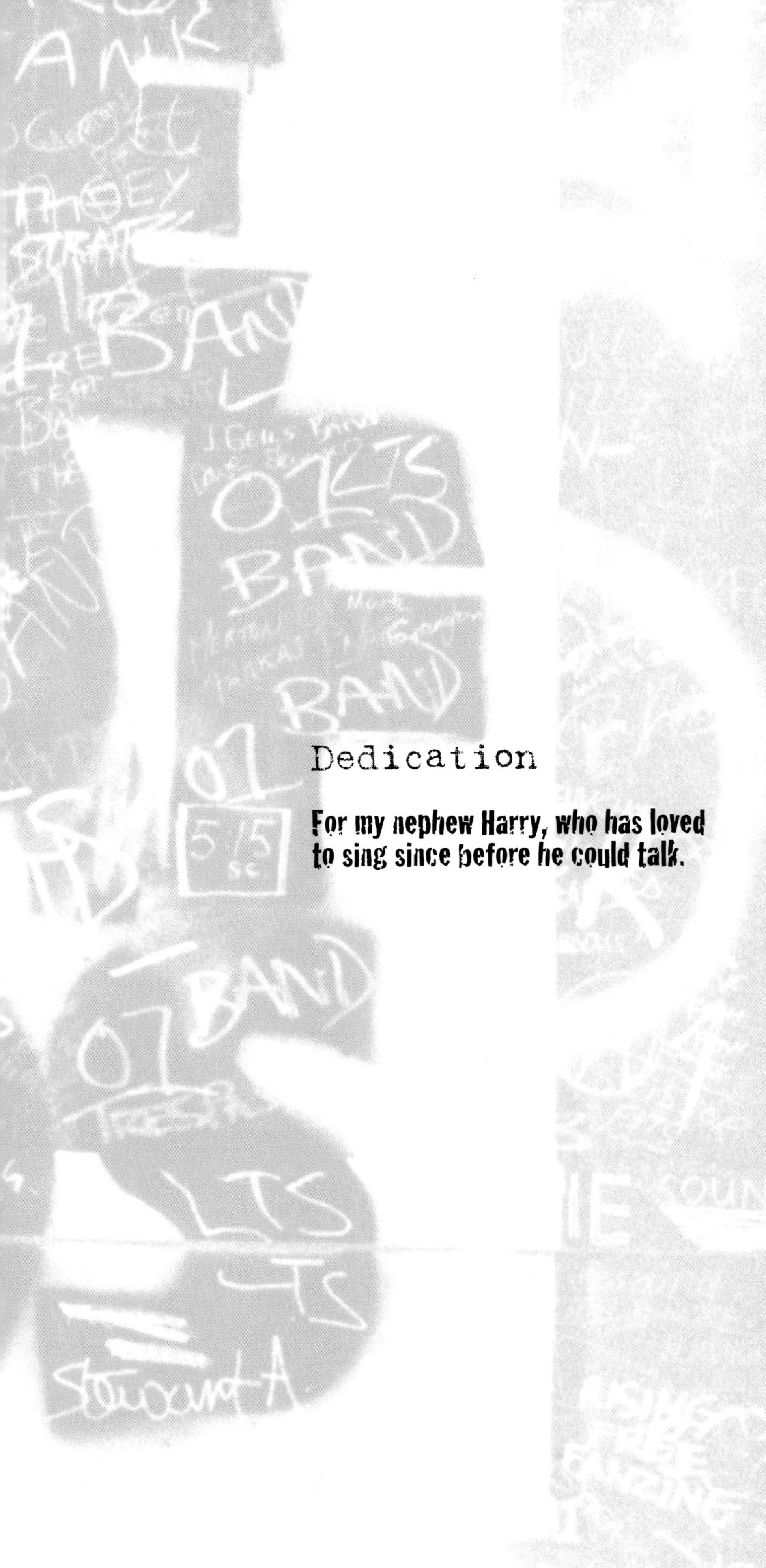

Dedication

For my nephew Harry, who has loved to sing since before he could talk.

SAL MINEO
"DINO"
BRIAN KEITH
SUSAN KOHNER
JOE DESANTIS
REGINALD ROSE

CONTENTS

Introduction

New wave, new romantic, electropop, power pop, post punk—the new music of the 1980s had about as many labels as it did influences. While the bands of this period took their cues from many diverse musical genres—disco, punk, Motown, reggae—most of them shared a similar pop music sensibility and an "anything goes" attitude toward the music industry. A far cry from the progressive, corporate rock of the 1970s, the 1980s sound was epitomized by a heavy dance beat, whirling synthesizers, catchy melodies, and soulful singing.

While a majority of these bands rose from the ashes of the punk rock movement, they owed as much to the self-indulgence of disco as they did to the angry protestations of punk. Image took precedence over everything. With heavy makeup, teased hair, and bizarre, eclectic costumes, bands such as A Flock of Seagulls, Human League, Duran Duran, Culture Club, and Depeche Mode emerged from the club scene in Great Britain and gained almost as much notoriety for their appearance as they did for their sound.

Aside from the inherent danceability of the music, the early 1980s bands owed a debt to disco for its fun-loving attitude, its dogged pursuit of androgyny, and its reliance on electronic sounds. From punk, the 1980s bands borrowed a desire to shock and the belief that rock and roll was a do-it-yourself art form open to anyone with the willingness to pick up an instrument and try to play it. In the mid-1970s bands, such as the Sex Pistols, the Clash, Talking Heads, and Elvis Costello and the Attractions opened up the debate over what constituted "good music." The progressive rock definition of "musicianship" took a back seat to passion, originality, and spontaneity. Bands started to take more chances and to experiment with different genres and different sounds, while at the same time simplifying their music and relying on tried-and-true pop melodies.

By the end of the 1970s and the beginning of the 1980s record companies had become much more open to alternative forms

Above: **David Byrne and Tina Weymouth of Talking Heads, one of the most influential and commercially successful bands to come out of the CBGB/New York punk rock scene.** Opposite: **In 1977, a bespectacled, nerdy Londoner named Elvis Costello (a.k.a. Declan McManus) burst onto the charts with his brash song writing and angry young man image.**

of music. This openness, however, was driven more by financial considerations than it was by any desire to be innovative. By 1980, record industry profits were declining. The minor financial successes and heavy media attention lavished on punk rock and new wave opened the eyes of many in the music industry who were now searching for the next big thing.

As the 1980s began, new wave crossover bands such as the Police, Tom Petty and the Heartbreakers, Talking Heads, and the Pretenders garnered major label contracts and moderate commercial success. Still, record companies were only willing to take chances on the more mainstream or established of the alternative bands. Then on August 1, 1981, Warner Communications and American Express launched a 24-hour cable channel called MTV. The station broadcast a nonstop format of music video clips introduced by a team of VJs (video jockeys). With its emphasis on the visual and a strong desire to provide an alternative to mainstream radio, MTV championed a new breed of musical artists. While bands like REO Speedwagon and Journey were ruling the radio waves, music television was breaking new ground promoting bands with strange names and even stranger looks. Culture Club, Duran Duran, Men at Work, Missing Persons, Orchestral Manoeuvers in the Dark (OMD), A Flock of Seagulls—it can be argued that MTV made these bands popular. On the other hand, if it were not for the new pop of the early 1980s, MTV may not have established itself as quickly as it did. These bands offered a sharp, yet commercially viable alternative to mainstream rock, which was beginning to bore the public and falter at the record stores. The new pop woke the listening public up. It was different, innovative, and fun. And, while not many of the bands had staying power, they did help to revitalize a sagging music industry while raising a few eyebrows and pricking up some ears.

From the Ashes of Punk

By the middle of the 1970s, rock and roll, which had been at the forefront of the popular music industry for more than twenty years, had begun a steady artistic decline. Most of the groundbreaking acts of the late 1960s had either left their best music behind them or had succumbed to the excesses of their own lifestyles. At the same time, the record industry began to consolidate at a steady pace, which meant that fewer labels were controlling a greater percentage of the profit. In rock and roll, the major record labels saw a cash cow. Profits from megabands such as Led Zeppelin, the Rolling Stones, Pink Floyd, Fleetwood Mac, Aerosmith, Bad Company, and a slew of their imitators were both steady and predictable. These bands could sell out fifty-thousand-seat stadiums while their yearly album releases were sure to race to the top of the *Billboard* charts. However, as the money continued to pour in, the industry became less and less willing to take creative chances.

Certainly, the history of rock and roll is full of many creative ebbs and flows. In the 1950s, rock and roll was characterized by raw emotion and dangerous energy. At first the movers and shakers of the popular music industry were skeptical of rock and roll, to say the least. Then RCA signed Elvis Presley, and everything changed. The major labels realized that there was money to be made, so they reluctantly went into the rock and roll business. However, by the end of the fifties, Elvis Presley was in the army, Buddy Holly was dead, the careers of Jerry Lee Lewis, Little Richard, and Chuck Berry were stalled by scandal, and the future of rock and roll was in jeopardy.

The major labels, who were never comfortable with the rebellious nature of the music, created their own watered-down, clean-cut version by propping up such teen heartthrob acts as Pat Boone, Ricky Nelson, Fabian, and Frankie Avalon. But, just as it seemed as

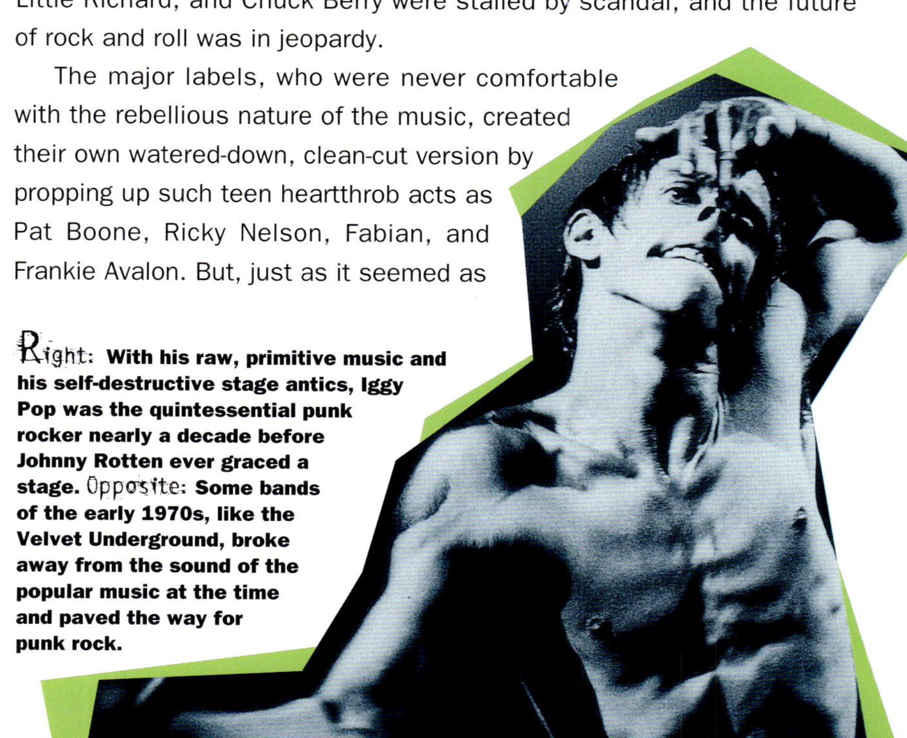

Right: With his raw, primitive music and his self-destructive stage antics, Iggy Pop was the quintessential punk rocker nearly a decade before Johnny Rotten ever graced a stage. Opposite: Some bands of the early 1970s, like the Velvet Underground, broke away from the sound of the popular music at the time and paved the way for punk rock.

though rock and roll was about to succumb to creative stagnation and mainstream mediocrity, in rushed the Beatles, the Rolling Stones, the Who, the Kinks, and the rest of the British Invasion. Soon Bob Dylan went electric, rock and roll became political, and bands began experimenting with new musical styles, nontraditional instruments, and inventive recording techniques.

By the early to mid 1970s, the idealism and experimentation that had sustained rock and roll through the 1960s was replaced by an artistically stifling obsession with the bottom line. As profits rose, the major labels got increasingly greedy and would only sign acts that they considered sure

things. The established moneymakers were given long-term contracts while chances were taken on new acts only when their music was well within the boundaries of what was already popular. At the same time, programming at the major radio stations around the country was influenced by a few high-powered consultants who also were more concerned with commercial viability than with musical creativity. AOR (album-oriented rock) radio playlists were shorter and more tightly controlled. The result of all of this was that as the seventies went on, rock became increasingly boring.

As popular music grew into a predictable, moneymaking dinosaur, a ragtag collection of young bands in New York City went back to basics with a stripped-down, mercurial sound that was a far cry from the art-rock pretensions of Pink Floyd and the macho posturing of Kiss. Taking their cue from the more esoteric acts of the late 1960s and early 1970s—the Velvet Underground, Iggy Pop and the Stooges,

MC5, New York Dolls, Jonathan Richman and the Modern Lovers, and Alex Chilton and Big Star; New York groups such as the Patti Smith Group, Television, The Ramones, Talking Heads, the Dictators, and Blondie; as well as Cleveland transplants Pere Ubu and the Dead Boys, developed a loyal cult following centered around a small club on the Bowery in New York City called CBGB. When these bands step-ped onstage, they relied more on attitude, emotion, satire, and seat-of-their-pants inspiration than they did on musical

Above: The New York Dolls were an outrageous glitter band whose image and legend were far more influential than their music. Opposite: Masters of the three-chord, two-minute rock song, The Ramones stayed true to their rock and roll roots in a career that lasted more than twenty years.

virtuosity, a philosophy that went against the progressive rock temperment that was rampant in commercial music at the time.

Perhaps the most influential, and certainly the longest-lasting group to come out of the New York art punk scene in the late 1970s was the long-haired, leather-clad Ramones. For the next twenty years, The Ramones would stick to their simple scorching version of 1960s garage rock, featuring deadpan, humorous lyrics, chainsaw guitars, and three-chord riffs. While churning out such prototypical punk songs as "Now I Wanna Sniff Some Glue," "Beat on the Brat," "Blitzkrieg Bop," and "Sheena Is a Punk Rocker," The Ramones epitomized the anything-goes,

I-can-do-that attitude that gave punk rock its energy and inspired countless future rock and rollers to strap on a guitar and strut their stuff.

One person who got caught up in the spirit of the New York punk scene was British boutique owner and former New York Dolls manager Malcolm McLaren. Born in London on January 26, 1946, McLaren has been both acclaimed as a postpunk visionary and derided as a controlling knave. In fact, both descriptions of this British art-school product are apropos McLaren was a master media manipulator who, by promoting alternative music and eccentric fashion, helped guide the British youth culture of the late 1970s and early 1980s.

McLaren was particularly fascinated by the young, volatile bass player for Television, Richard Hell. Born Richard Meyers from Lexington, Kentucky, Hell had played with Johnny Thunders (formerly of the New York Dolls) in the Heartbreakers and then with the Neon Boys, who eventually became Television. McLaren tried to convince Hell to come back to London with him and start a band. Hell declined the offer and stayed in New York to start up his own band, the Voidoids.

Undeterred by Hell's rejection, McLaren went back to London and opened up a clothing shop called Sex, specializing in "antifashion"—clothing inspired by the Teddy Boy look of the 1950s and the same torn, safety pin–strewn clothing that Richard Hell was wearing back in New York. McLaren's vision proved popular in economically stressed London, leading McLaren to further his vision by creating a band to fit his fashion. He recruited a part-time employee of Sex, Glen Matlock, and

Matlock's two friends Paul Cook and Steve Jones, and then asked a nineteen-year-old neighborhood punk named John Lydon to sing. Jones later dubbed the rude yet charismatic singer Johnny Rotten, allegedly because of his disregard for personal hygiene. Rotten's friend Sid Vicious replaced Matlock in 1977 when Matlock's perceived direction for the band wasn't the same as the other members'. He left to form Rich Kids, and the Sex Pistols went on to become one of the most infamous bands of the punk-rock era.

Manager and promoter extraordinaire Malcom McLaren (left) with drummer Paul Cook of the Sex Pistols.

Right: Steve Jones, Sid Vicious, Johnny Rotten, and Paul Cook lasted only two years as the Sex Pistols, but had a lasting impact on rock and roll. Below: Ari Up, lead singer of the Slits, the first all-female band of the British punk scene. Ari was only 14 years old when the Slits played their first gig.

In their brief but meteoric two-year existence, the Sex Pistols proved to be one of the most influential bands of the 1970s, and their one and only release as a band, *Never Mind the Bollocks, Here's the Sex Pistols*, ranks as one of the most important rock and roll albums ever. Through sophisticated hype (carefully orchestrated by McLaren), a raw, snarling sound (rooted in basic garage rock and roll), and cutting, often offensive politically minded lyrics (courtesy of Johnny Rotten), the Sex Pistols put the danger back into rock and roll and inspired an entire youth movement in England. Bands such as the Clash, the Damned, the Buzzcocks, Siouxsie and the Banshees, the Slits, and The Jam sprang up along with and in the wake of the Sex Pistols, forming one of the most vital and prolific periods in British rock and roll history.

Above: **Led by a sultry Debbie Harry, Blondie was one of the first bands to be called new wave.** Opposite: **From Boston, the Cars were one of the most successful new wave bands of the late seventies and early eighties. Their first two albums, *The Cars* and *Candy-O*, sold more than six million copies. This shot is from the video for one of their biggest hits, "You Might Think."**

This generation of working-class youth rejected the institutionalized "rock star" establishment (Rod Stewart was an easy and frequent target of British punks) and was wary of major record labels (a feeling that was mutual at the time). This was do-it-yourself music, often based as much on fashion and raw emotion as it was on musical ability. Thus, a slew of small independent record labels sprang up to fill the growing demand. At the same time, a tightly knit network of home-produced "fanzines" spread the word about the latest bands and trends.

Punk rock was much slower to catch on in the United States. There were scenes centered in New York, Los Angeles, Cleveland, Austin, Washington, D.C., and other major cities, but for the most part, punk in the United States was watered down into what would at the time be called new wave, an extremely overused umbrella term that included just about every new band from the late seventies that sounded even the slightest bit original. Talking Heads, Tom Petty, the Cars, Mink Deville, the Motels, Blondie, and the Pretenders were just a few of the bands to be collared with this label.

It is out of the ashes of punk rock and early new wave that the new sound of the early 1980s, new wave or new pop, rose. The Sex Pistols, the Clash, and the Jam played to packed London clubs whose crowds included Adam Ant, George O'Dowd, Dave Gahan, Gary Numan, and Andy Taylor. It was these musicians who would smooth out the edges of punk, add a danceable backbeat, and throw a catchy melody on top, creating the new wave sound of the early 1980s. As punk rock flamed out, a

Below: **The Jam took their cues from the mods and the Merseybeat of the 1960s.** Opposite: **Rebels with a cause—Joe Strummer, and Paul Simonon, Mick Jones, and Topper Headon comprised the Clash, a British band that channeled the anger of punk into innovative music with a political agenda.**

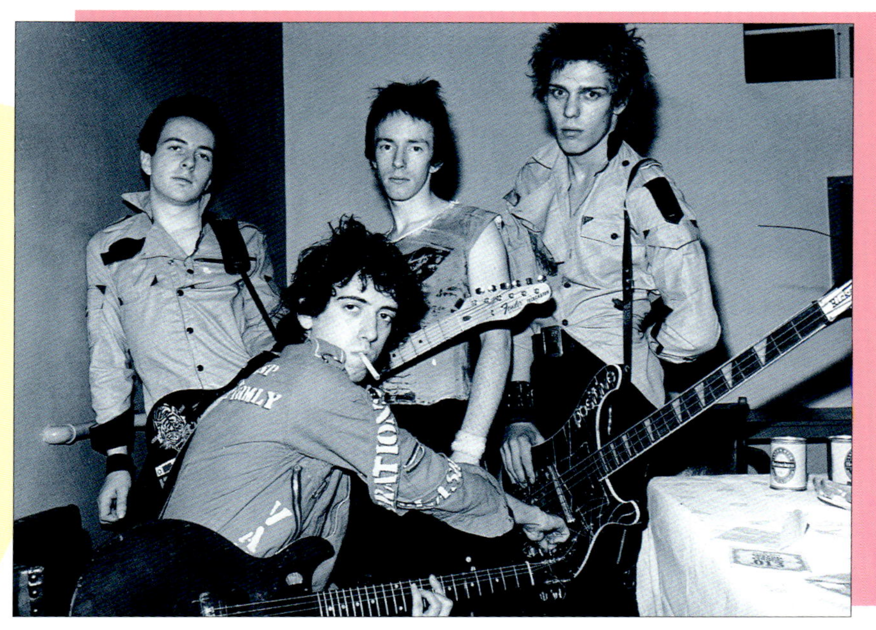

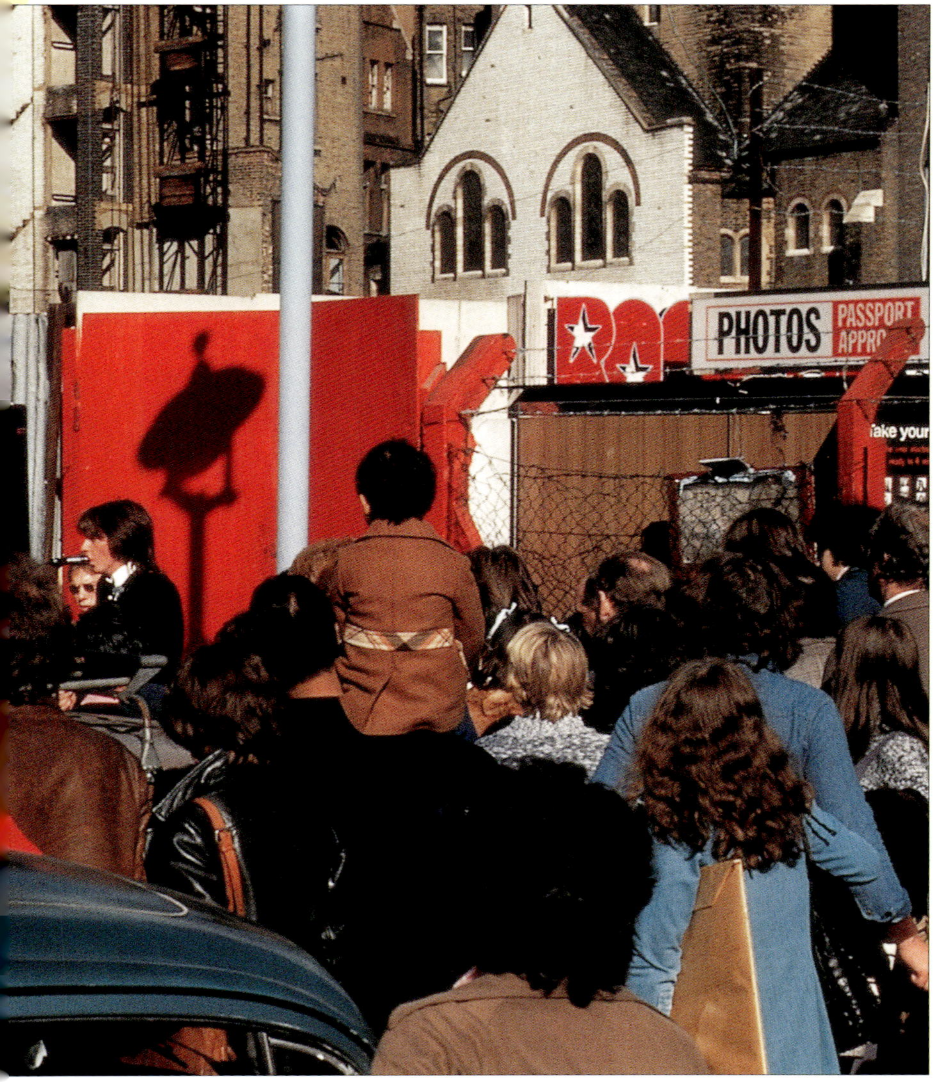
PHOTOS
PASSPORT
Take your

Dale Bozio of Missing Persons decked out in the outrageous fashion of the early 1980s.

second wave of British youth picked up the slack and created their own scene centered around the London nightclubs and discos. Whereas punk was driven by raw energy, confrontation, and a pessimistic outlook, the new pop would depend on outrageous fashion, visual interest, and the desire to have a good time. And these previously unknown faces would be beamed into millions of living rooms via a new television medium that would forever change the face of rock and roll and turn around the stagnant record industry.

The Romantics

On St. Valentine's Day in 1977, four factory workers from Detroit, Michigan, joined forces to form a powerpop/new wave quartet called the Romantics. Wearing matching leather outfits—usually red, black, or pink—Wally Palmer (vocals, guitar), Mike Skill (guitar, vocals), Rich Cole (bass, vocals), and Jimmy Marinos (drums, vocals) extensively toured the East Coast club scene with jangling guitars, throwaway lyrics, and a heavy back beat. In 1978, they released their first single, "Little White Lies" backed with "I Can't Tell You Anything," on their own label, Spider Records. The single ended up on the desk of rock critic Greg Shaw, whose ear was caught by the Romantics' up-tempo pop sound. The band signed with Shaw's newly formed Bomp! label and released the single " I Tell it to Carrie" in 1978.

In 1979, the Romantics signed with Nemperor Records and a year later released their first album, *The Romantics.* The album reached number 61 on the *Billboard* charts and featured a minor hit titled "What I Like About You," which peaked at number 49 in 1980. While the song was very popular on college radio, it did not become popular in the mainstream until several years later when it was licensed (without the band's permission) for use in advertisements for Budweiser beer, Home Box Office, and several other products.

The Romantics' next two albums, *National Breakout* (1980) and *Strictly Personal* (1981) stayed true to the band's sound, but neither one cracked the top 100 on the *Billboard* charts. In 1983, the band reassessed their image and their sound. They did away with their new wave outfits and their trademark three-minute, power-pop tunes and turned to a more traditional commercial-rock sound that was more at home in arena-sized venues than it was in new wave clubs. The about-face breathed new life into the band, and their fourth album *In Heat* (1983) turned out to be their most successful, peaking at number 14, thanks largely to the hit single, "Talking In Your Sleep" (number two, 1983).

Despite the Romantics' new-found success, drummer Jimmy Marinos—who sang lead on "What I Like About You"—quit the band in 1983. He was replaced by drummer David Patratos, who played on their 1985 album *Rhythm Romance.* Patratos was then replace d by ex-Blondie drummer Clem Burke in 1989, but the band broke up soon after. In 1990, Epic records released a best-of album entitled *What I Like About You (and Other Romantic Hits).*

The Romantics

The New Romantics

Because of the drastic decline in record sales from the industry's peak in 1978 to 1979, record execs knew it was time to look for "the next big thing." The philosophy of sticking with proven acts had started to backfire: the younger record-buying public was bored with the music currently dominating the air waves and the older core audience was outgrowing its taste for classic rock. While punk rock had little economic impact in the United States, it did wake up the record industry and spark a whole new wave of music.

The first wave, the new romantics, made up a short-lived pop movement that was centered around London clubs such as Billy's in SoHo and the Blitz in Covent Garden. The chief promoters of this highly fashion-conscious scene were shop assistant–turned–professional socialite Steve Strange and former Rich Kids drummer Rusty Egan, who hosted weekly "Heroes Nights" at various clubs around town. These events attracted punks, art students, mods, soul boys, transvestites, and any other manner of eccentric who wasn't shy with makeup and who enjoyed dressing up in frilly shirts, colorful frocks, and outrageous hats. In the new romantic fashion, just about any style from any period was fine as long as it was obscure, mismatched, and flamboyant.

The fad never really took off commercially because it lacked a focused, marketable look and its chief practitioners disavowed any label (Futurists, the New Dandies) that was attached to it. Still, out of the London club scene sprang a number of important bands that would pave the way for the pop explosion of the 1980s.

The first of the new romantics to enter the mainstream was London native Stuart

Above: Adam and the Ants were one of the first new romantic bands to come out of London's post-punk club scene. Opposite: After working as a roadie for Generation X and playing briefly with Chrissie Hynde in Moors Murderers, Steve Strange became a promoter at two British new romantic clubs, Billy's and the Blitz. He later formed Visage with Rusty Egan and Midge Ure.

Leslie Goddard, otherwise known as Adam Ant. Ant had a unique fashion sense that combined the clothing and images of pirates, cowboys, and Indians into a new romantic "Prince Charming" look. He described his heavily African-rhythmed music as "Ant music for sex people," and described his fans as "Ant People."

Ant had been hanging around the fringes of the London punk scene since 1976, working briefly in various unknown bands and then with Adam and the Ants. It was not until he came under the wing of former Sex Pistols manager Malcolm McLaren that Ant enjoyed any type of commercial success. Combining an unusual, yet highly danceable, double-drum Burundi beat with yodeling vocals and the singer's own "Ant" vocabulary, Adam and the Ants came to national attention in Great Britain with the release of their first album, *Dirk Wears White Sox*, in 1979. One year later, however, a fight for control of the band caused Malcolm McLaren to split with Ant, and to make matters worse, he took

From left to right: **Annabella Lwin, Leroy Gorman, Matthew Ashman, and David Barberossa of Bow Wow Wow, a Malcom McLaren project that scored top ten hits with "Wild in the Country" and a remake of the Strangeloves' "I Want Candy."**

the singer's backing band members—David Barberossa, Matthew Ashmen, and Andrew Warren—with him for his next band project, Bow Wow Wow.

Far from being defeated by McLaren's betrayal, Ant thrived. He teamed up with former Rema Rema and Models guitar player Marco Pirroni to write the songs for the 1980 release *Kings of the Wild Frontier*,

Left: Con man, innovator, charlatan, or Andy Warhol of the post-punk scene—Malcom McLaren was a ubiquitous figure in the 1970s and 1980s music scene, having figured into the careers of the New York Dolls, the Sex Pistols, Chrissie Hynde, Adam Ant, Bow Wow Wow, Boy George, and the Damned. Opposite: Two of the three Thompson Twins, Tom Bailey and Alannah Currie.

which quickly rose to number one on the British charts. He followed that with 1981's *Prince Charming*, which spent more than six months on the British charts.

Despite a major media blitz and a well-publicized tour, Adam and the Ant's music never really took off in the United States. The new Ants disbanded in 1982 and Adam Ant released his solo album *Friend or Foe*, which gave him his only success in the U.S.—the MTV hit and number twelve single "Goody Two Shoes."

While Adam was enjoying success with his new Ants, McLaren took the one-time band members and the Burundi beat and sound added a fourteen-year-old Burmese dry-cleaner clerk named Annabella Lwin (born Myant Myant Aye in Rangoon, Burma) to form Bow Wow Wow. Although she had no previous experience, Annabella had the exotic look and sexy squeal to complement Bow Wow Wow's blend of Gary Glitter–inspired African rhythms, new romantic pop, and surf instrumentals.

In 1980, the band signed with EMI and released the single "C30, C60, C90 Go!," which recommended that people illegally tape music off the air. This was followed by the twenty-minute, eight-second song *Your Cassette Pet*, available only in cassette format. Never a stranger to controversy, McLaren came under fire for promoting child pornography for having a scantily clad then fifteen-year-old Lwin sing songs such as "Sexy Eiffel Tower," which cited the structure as a large phallic symbol. EMI dropped the band, but they were quickly picked up by RCA.

Just as Bow Wow Wow was about to release their debut album and embark on a U.S. tour, Annabella's mother (who was always against Annabella's singing career) called Scotland Yard and alleged that the young girl was being exploited for immoral purposes. The band would only be allowed to leave for the United States if McLaren and RCA promised *not* to publish a nude photo of Annabella based on the Manet painting *Déjeuner sur l'Herbe*. McLaren agreed to the terms. The band left for their tour and Bow Wow Wow's first album, *See Jungle! See Jungle! Go Join Your Gang, Yeah, City All Over! Go Ape Crazy!*, was released in both the United States and Great Britain with the nude photo of Annabella on the cover. Because he wanted to control and hold onto his controversial hot new star, McLaren intimidated Annabella by threatening to replace her with Boy George before George became famous with Culture Club (see page 32).

Perhaps the one band that most ardently embraced the new romantic label was Duran Duran. Named after a character in the Jane Fonda–Roger Vadim sci-fi spoof *Barbarella*, Duran Duran played an accessible mixture of new wave and disco. Believing that style was at least as important as music, the members of Duran Duran teased their hair, applied heavy makeup, wore trend-setting parachute clothing, and positioned themselves as sexy young playboys. They scored their first hit in Europe with the disco-pop single "Planet Earth," but didn't enjoy success in the United States until the advent of MTV (see chapter three).

Above: **With their bubblegum soul, dance-pop sound, Haircut 100 hit the U.S. Top 40 in 1982 with the single "Love Plus One."** Opposite: **The quintessential technopop band of the 1980s, Depeche Mode used synthesizers and drum machines to create a stark, moody sound with plenty of hooks. Their name was inspired by a French fashion magazine.**

Although a number of bands that would make significant contributions to the new pop sound of the early eighties were briefly aligned with the new romantic movement—Spandau Ballet, ABC, Haircut 100, Soft Cell, Depeche Mode, and the Thompson Twins—the movement itself was extremely short-lived and never truly caught on outside a few clubs in London and Hollywood. But it was important because it did help define some of the early characteristics of the new pop wave of the early eighties: it celebrated the importance of image and fashion; it added a danceable beat and catchy melodies to new music; and it stressed humor and quirkiness over politics and confrontation. And, most importantly, some of the musicians arose from this movement are revered as icons of new wave.

Culture Club and Boy George

No other band epitomized the sound, attitude, and look of the new pop of the early 1980ss better than Culture Club. Led by the flamboyant and charismatic Boy George, Culture Club rose to the top of charts thanks to eclectic, hook-laden music, spirited music videos, and a sincere—if unusual—public persona.

With his androgynous looks, soulful voice, and capricious attitude, Boy George was a poster boy for the image-conscious eighties. When the band first came to prominence, George was looked on askance by a general public that didn't know what to make of his bizarre appearance—frilly frocks, heavy makeup, and Hasidic hat. But George turned out to be a likeable, talkative misfit who was eventually embraced by the mainstream and became a regular on American television talk shows. (George even developed a close friendship with Joan Rivers.)

Born George Alan O'Dowd in 1961, Boy George was a product of the post-punk, new romantic club scene in London in the late 1970s and early 1980s. He held various odd jobs, but what he truly lived for was the effulgence of the London nightlife at clubs such as Billy's in SoHo and the Blitz in Covent Garden.

One night while at Planets, Boy George saw Malcolm McLaren, who had just formed Bow Wow Wow. George had heard through the grapevine that McLaren was threatening to replace Annabella with another singer. Wearing stilettos and a straw hat with birds on it, George drunkenly introduced himself to McLaren and announced, "I want to sing with Bow Wow Wow." McLaren hired George, who briefly sang with the band as "Lieutenant Lush."

While Boy George was aspiring to become part of the music scene through Bow Wow Wow, bassist Mikey Craig was making the rounds in Bristol, jumping from one band to another. As his frustration grew with the failure of each band, Craig realized that if he wanted to get anywhere, he needed to form a band of his own. Seeing potential in the odd-looking George,

George Alan O'Dowd, a.k.a. Boy George, of Culture Club.

Craig arranged to meet him and the two immediately hit it off. George teamed up with a guitar player named Suede, and decided to name their new band Sex Gang Children. George's boyfriend, musician Kirk Brandon of Theatre of Hate, introduced him to drummer Jon Moss, who had played with the Damned and Adam and the Ants. Moss was an extremely savvy and driven musician who had grown tired of the British punk scene and wanted to write and perform songs that would appeal to a wide audience—trendy club kids as well as their parents. They changed the name of the band to Caravan Club, then Can't Wait Club, and finally to Culture Club.

EMI, who had been interested in Boy George since his brief stint with Bow Wow Wow, paid for a demo of two songs: "Eyes of Medusa" and "I'm an Animal." Both the band and EMI were disappointed in the tapes. At the urging of Moss, they fired Suede and, after auditioning dozens of strummers, hired Roy Hay, who also doubled on keyboards. Culture Club played their first gig at Croc's in Rayleigh, Essex, the home of Depeche Mode.

After weighing offers from several record companies, the band finally settled on Virgin and released their debut album, *Kissing to Be Clever* in 1983. Produced by Steve Levine, the album yielded several massive hits on both sides of the Atlantic: "Do You Really Want to Hurt Me" (number one U.K., number two U.S.), "I'll Tumble 4 Ya" (number one U.K., number nine U.S.), and "Time (Clock of the Heart)" (number three U.K., number two U.S.). They quickly followed up their debut success by releasing *Colour by Numbers* at the end of 1983. This second album reached number two on the U.S. charts and yielded five top twenty hits, "Church of the Poison Mind," "Victims," "It's a Miracle," "Miss Me Blind," and their top-selling single, "Karma Chameleon," which hit number one in both the United States and Great Britain. The successes of these two albums led to a Grammy Award for the Best New Artist of 1983.

With their videos in heavy rotation on the fledgling MTV (see chapter three) and an eager media thirsting after their peculiar lead singer, Culture Club seemed to be everywhere. But due to a combination of overexposure and a lack of quality songs, Culture Club's 1984 album, *Waking Up with the House on Fire*, was a critical and commercial disappointment, reaching only number twenty-six on the charts. It seemed as though even Boy George was growing tired of Boy George. He cut his hair and grew stubble. The low point for the band came when they played at the 1985 Athens European Culture Festival and the crowd threw bricks.

In 1986, Culture Club released the aptly titled *From Luxury to Heartache*. A few months later, a police raid on his house forced George to publicly admit to his heroin problem. He was arrested for possession of narcotics and went into rehab. Later that year a musician named Michael Rudetsky died of a drug overdose in George's home. The singer was cleared of charges implicating him in the death and he went back into rehab. Flagging sales and George's personal problems led the band to break up that year.

Boy George released three solo albums over the next seven years and scored a few minor hits on the European dance circuit, but mainstream popularity eluded him until he recorded a cover of Dave Berry's 1964 hit "The Crying Game" for the 1992 hit movie of the same name. In 1995, George released his fourth solo album, *Cheapness and Beauty*, and wrote a revealing autobiography entitled *Take It Like a Man*.

MTV and the New British Invasion

On August 1, 1981, at 12:01 A.M. Eastern Standard Time, a new twenty-four-hour cable television "visual radio" station went on the air with an appropriate video—"Video Killed the Radio Star" by the Buggles. Few people involved with Music Television (MTV) at the time could have predicted how strong an impact the fledgling cable channel would have, not only on the music industry, but on television, film, advertising, and a whole generation.

Targeted at twelve- to thirty-four-year-olds and hosted by unknown actors and established radio personalities acting as VJs (as opposed to DJs), the station aired a new art form called the music video: a short, visual interpretation of a song that was used to promote artists (see page 36). When it signed on the air, MTV had a minuscule budget of $20 million and a library of fewer than three hundred videos, thirty of which were by Rod Stewart. MTV was eventually able to convince the major record companies to bankroll the promotional videos and provide them to the station for free, promising that exposure through the cable channel would lead to increased record sales.

Through its first few years, MTV operated in the red, but its creators had enough confidence in its future to keep it bankrolled. Gradually MTV expanded to larger cable markets and refined its format, and in the process drastically changed the popular music landscape. After just two years in existence, MTV was carried by 1,775 cable operators, making it the fastest-growing network in cable television

Above: The fashion-conscious Duran Duran emerged from the British new romantic movement to worldwide fame largely on the basis of their music videos on MTV. Opposite: The Buggles (Geoffry Downes and Trevor Horn) inaugurated MTV with their hit "Video Killed the Radio Star." The producer/musician duo later went on to join the progressive rock band Yes in March of 1980.

history. Virtually every artist who received MTV airtime enjoyed a sharp rise in record sales. Bands that were previously completely unknown to the American public, such as Duran Duran and Men at Work, were suddenly topping the charts, almost exclusively because of their exposure on MTV.

Because the music video is primarily a visual medium—the music is often secondary to the images—the bands that enjoyed early successes on MTV were those that had cultivated an interesting or unusual look

A Brief History of the Music Video

The explosion of music video channels such as MTV and VH-1 have inextricably joined popular music and the moving image. But the truth is that music and film have been used hand in hand since the invention of the movie camera.

While nearly all early theatrical films were produced with elaborate movie scores that enhanced the drama and action on the screen, the music video dates back to 1921 and the work of Oskar Fischinger, a German filmmaker and composer who was a pioneer at combining music and images. Before Fischinger, music had been added to films to support the visuals. Fischinger was the first person to reverse the process and create animated shorts to support jazz and classical records. Many of his films were used as advertisements; like today's music videos, their purpose was primarily for promotion.

In 1940, Walt Disney, with the aid of Oskar Fischinger, produced the landmark animated film *Fantasia*, which can be considered the first long-form music video, with cartoon images set to famous classical

The original MTV VJs (from left to right): Alan Hunter, Martha Quinn, Mark Goodman, Nina Blackwood, and J.J. Jackson.

music scores. *Fantasia* was also the first movie to use multichannel stereophonic sound. Later in the decade, a video jukebox called the Panoram Soundie was developed to bring music videos to a wide audience. While most of the music clips offered on the Soundie machines were excerpts from Hollywood musicals, many short films of musicians such as Bing Crosby, Cab Calloway, and Louis Armstrong were produced specifically for the video jukeboxes. Unfortunately, each Soundie was extremely heavy (weighing up to two tons [1.8t]), was prone to breakdowns, and could play only one film at a time. By the time television had become mainstream in the 1950s, the Soundie was obsolete. Later in the 1950s, a French company developed a much smaller video jukebox called the Scopitone, which could play up to thirty-six films. This machine lasted well into the 1960s before the novelty wore off.

Television was to be the medium that would eventually popularize the music video. In the 1950s, television variety shows such as *The Ed Sullivan Show* and *The Steve Allen Show* had regular segments featuring live rock and roll acts. Shows such as *Your Hit Parade, American Bandstand,* and *TV Teen Club* were exclusively dedicated to music and dance. The lineage of the modern-day music video can also be traced to the rock and roll movies of Elvis Presley and the Beatles, as well as the 1950s rock and roll hit film *The Girl Can't Help It,* which featured performances by Little Richard, Eddie Cochran, Gene Vincent, Fats Domino, and the Platters.

In 1965, executives from Columbia developed a television show based on a band of wacky, fun-loving moptops who lived together and went on weekly adventures that were interspersed with musical interludes. *The Monkees,* which debuted in the fall of 1966, was a direct response to the success of the Beatles movie *A Hard Day's Night.* Top songwriters were hired to write hit songs for this fictitious band, and records were made to promote the show on the Top 40 charts. The singles, in turn, were promoted by at least one musical segment during each half-hour show.

Throughout the 1960s and early 1970s, bands such as the Beatles, the Kinks, Procol Harum, and countless others used videos to promote their music in areas where they were not touring. In Great Britain, shows such as *Top of the Pops* eagerly aired promotional videos of bands that could not appear live. In the United States, however, any pop-oriented shows that relied on the video format failed miserably.

The first quantifiable video-generated hit came in 1975. Queen had recorded a brilliant but unusual single called "Bohemian Rhapsody," but because of the length of the song and the peculiar nature of its construction, the band decided it needed some sort of promotional vehicle to get the song noticed and played. They hired Bruce Gofers and spent $7,000 and two days shooting a kinetic and aptly theatrical video for the song. The clip was then distributed to television shows, clubs, and record stores across the United States and Great Britain, and the song became one of the most enduring hits of the 1970s.

After the success of "Bohemian Rhapsody," bands and record companies on both sides of the Atlantic started to realize the promotional value of the music video. Still, there were very few television shows or other video outlets to which they could distribute these clips. Then in 1980, Warner Communications and American Express created the Amex Satellite Entertainment Corporation. One of the first projects proposed by company president John Lack was for a twenty-four-hour music video channel. Thus, MTV was born.

Above: Dave Stewart and Annie Lennox of the Eurythmics. With Lennox's soulful vocals and Stewart's studio wizardry, the Eurythmics were the most creative and enduring of the 1980s synth-pop bands. Opposite: Soft Cell made it big with their still-popular hit, "Tainted Love."

and who already had some experience in making music videos (or clips, as they were originally called). Artists who were less "videogenic" or were slow to embrace the video format often missed out—a reversal of what happened to silent-screen stars when "talkies" appeared. (Actors who looked great onscreen but did not have the right voice or vocal delivery were left behind when sound movies became the rage.) In the early 1980s, if a musician did not have an unusual look or a highly cultivated image, he or she was not going to enjoy the opportunities that MTV offered, no matter how good his or her music was.

In the musical climate shift caused by MTV, the British new pop bands had a distinct advantage over their American counterparts. Coming as they did out of the British club scene and partially inspired—at least in fashion—by the punk movement, bands such as A Flock of Seagulls, the Eurythmics, Soft Cell, ABC, and Duran Duran had the coifed look, whimsical fashions, and sci-fi attitude that would play well on MTV. In addition, many of these bands had already been making music videos shown on highly popular British performance shows such as *Top of the Pops*. Christened the "New British Invasion," this loosely knit group of androgynous, image-centered stars dominated the television airwaves in the early 1980s and gave birth to term "MTV Band."

The first of the new pop bands to hit it big through MTV was Duran Duran. With their teen-idol looks and keyboard-oriented, disco-rock-pop sounds, Duran Duran had become hugely popular in England, Australia, and Europe. Fame in the United States, however, eluded them at first. They spent months touring clubs in the United States and doing interviews for the music rags, but their first two albums, *Duran Duran* (1981) and *Rio* (1982) were commercial flops in America. Part of the problem was that the band couldn't get any airplay outside of the popular new-wave station KROQ in Los Angeles. Seeing MTV as their last great opportunity, the band hired directors Kevin Gogley and Lol Creme (formerly of 10cc) to direct a sex-filled video (complete with nude women wrestling in oil) for their song "Girls on Film." For the *Rio* album, the band flew to Sri Lanka to shoot videos for "Hungry Like the Wolf," "Save a Prayer," "Is There Something I Should Know," and "Rio." All four of these videos

The Go-Go's

In 1978, an all-girl, punk novelty act took the stage at the Hollywood punk club the Masque. Crashing through an extremely short set that consisted of one and a half songs, the band garnered more smiles and laughter then respect. A few years later, however, the Go-Go's would be playing arenas instead of punk dives, topping the charts with a number-one debut album, *Beauty and the Beat*, and two top-twenty singles, "Our Lips Are Sealed" and "We Got the Beat."

The Go-Go's began when a former high school cheerleader and punk-scene regular named Belinda Carlisle started playing guitar and writing songs with

The Go-Go's started as an Los Angeles punk band, but gained fame playing powerpop.

another punk-scene stalwart, Jane Wiedlin. Carlisle had briefly been involved with the bands Black Randy and the Metro Squad, and had nearly joined the seminal L.A. hardcore band the Germs. Carlisle and Wiedlin were joined by the more experienced guitar player Charlotte Caffey, bassist Margot Olaverra, and drummer Elissa Bello.

The more they rehearsed, the more seriously they started taking themselves and they soon replaced Bello with drummer Gina Schock, who had toured briefly with cult movie star Edie Massey and her Eggs. Gradually the Go-Go's sound changed from hard-driving punk to catchy powerpop. Things weren't happening for them in L.A., so the band went to England in 1979 where they toured with the British Ska band Madness. While in England, the all-girl band cut a version of "We Got the Beat" for Stiff Records, which became a marginal hit in British and American new-wave dance clubs. After returning to the United States, Olaverra became ill and left the band. She was replaced with Kathy Valentine, formerly of the all-girl metal band Girlschool.

In 1981, the band signed with I.R.S., who lined up veteran girl-group producer Richard Gottehrer. Gottehrer had written and produced many girl-group hits in the 1960s, including "My Boyfriend's Back" by the Angels (number one in 1963). He later worked with the Climax Blues Band, Joan Armatrading, and Blondie. By the spring of 1982, *Beauty and the Beat* hit number one, where it stayed for six weeks, making the Go-Go's the first all-girl band to score a number one album. The band was very popular on MTV, and they were invited to play at the first MTV birthday party on-air concert. That same year they toured with the equally hot A Flock of Seagulls.

The Go-Go's quickly followed up their successful debut with 1982's *Vacation.* That album peaked at number eight and had a top-ten single with the title cut. Their third album, *Talk Show* (1984), was a disappointment, reaching only number eighteen with the minor hit singles "Head Over Heels" and "Turn to You." Internal strife and artistic differences led to Wiedlin leaving the band, and the Go-Go's broke up soon after.

Carlisle enjoyed a successful solo career with the release of *Belinda* in 1986. The album, which featured the playing of Wiedlin and Caffey, went gold, reaching number thirteen on the charts. Her next effort, *Heaven on Earth* (1987), went platinum and had major hits with "Heaven Is a Place on Earth" (number one), "I Get Weak" (number two), and "Circle in the Sand" (number seven).

The Go-Go's reunited briefly in 1990 to promote a greatest hits album, and then recorded an album of new material, *Return to the Valley of the Go-Go's*, in 1994.

featured exotic locales, attractive women, and the handsome young gents doing exciting things like sailing on a yacht and stalking through the jungle. In terms of quality, visual interest, and imagination, these videos were far above the average performance-oriented video shown on MTV. After their videos received heavy rotation on MTV, *Rio*, once thought dead in the water, climbed the *Billboard* charts and cracked the top twenty, with the single "Hungry Like the Wolf" peaking at number three.

Another British new pop band to ride MTV to the top of the charts was A Flock of Seagulls. Formed in 1980 by hairdresser Mike Score, his brother Ali, salon assistant Frank Maudsley, and guitar player Paul Reynolds, this Liverpudlian band played a sci-fi-influenced brand of synthesized Eurodisco but is perhaps best remembered for Mike Score's unforgettable peroxide blonde, cascading haircut. The band's first single, "Telecommunication," was a minor hit in with European club scene and among a few of the trendier clubs in New York and Los Angeles. With the release of their self-titled debut album in 1982, the band headed to the United States for a brief tour with hopes of making it big. To promote the band, their record company, Arista, delivered a video for the single "I Ran" to MTV. The song was a simple pop melody with a catchy hook, recorded with echoey layers of synthesizer and a simple electronic drumbeat. The video showed the band in all of their sci-fi glory—flowing

Above: **Slim Jim Phantom, Brian Setzer, and Lee Rocker of the Stray Cats. This neo-rockabilly band sold more than two million copies of their first album, *Built for Speed*, thanks largely to the success of the music videos for "Rock this Town" and "Stray Cat Strut."** Opposite: **A Flock of Seagulls lead singer Mike Score's distinctive hair-dos were emblematic of the 1980s new pop.**

hair, silver jumpsuits, and funny sung asses—and featured spinning cameras and a futuristic set. Les Garland of MTV liked the video and the channel immediately put it into heavy rotation. Within a few weeks "I Ran" was in the top ten, and this unheralded band's debut album hit the top twenty.

British bands, however, were not the only ones to ride the MTV bandwagon to the top of the charts. The Australian pop phenomenon Men at Work (see page 44), the Long Island rockabilly revival band the Stray Cats, and the all-girl, postpunk, powerpop band the Go-Go's (see page 40) also hit it big on both television and radio. The Stray Cats became so dependent on their MTV success that on their North American tour, they played only those areas where the cable station was being carried. The Go-Go's went from playing a one-and-a-half-song punk set at Hollywood's Masque in 1978 to being the queens of powerpop when their debut album, *Beauty and the Beat*, hit number one in the United States on the strength of the singles "We Got the Beat" and "Our Lips Are Sealed."

But not every band that received heavy play from MTV became a long-lasting pop legend. The history of the channel is full of groups who made a small splash with one or two videos but were never heard from again. A

Men at Work

The early 1980s produced more than its share of bands that enjoyed sudden, overwhelming success but then quickly disappeared off the radar screen. It was a time when the music industry was in flux, and everyone—fans and music executives alike—was looking for the next big thing.

In 1982, an obscure Australian band called Men at Work stormed onto the *Billboard* charts with an LP full of catchy tunes and a handful of funny music videos. That year, *Business as Usual* was number one for fifteen weeks, breaking the Monkees' 1966 record for the longest run at number one for a debut album. In addition, *Business as Usual* and the smash single "Down Under" topped both the U.S. and U.K. single and album charts at the same time—a feat no one had achieved since Rod Stewart did it in 1972 with the single "Maggie May," and the album it appears on, *Every Picture Tells a Story*.

Men at Work formed in 1979 when a twenty-six-year-old Scottish-born singer named Colin Hay joined up with local Melbourne musicians Ron Strykert (guitar), Jerry Speiser (drums), Greg Ham (sax, flute, keyboards), and John Rees (bass). The band toiled on the Australian pub scene for three years—gaining a large following from regular gigs at the Cricketer's Arms Hotel—before signing with Australian Columbia. *Business as Usual* shot to number one in Australia and stayed there for ten weeks. Their success down under led Columbia to promote them in the United States. After the band's successful tour opening for Fleetwood Mac and with their zany videos in heavy rotation on MTV, *Business as Usual* stormed up the U.S. charts and stayed there for almost two years, producing two number one singles, "Land Down Under" and "Who Can It Be Now?" In addition, the band won a Grammy Award for Best New Artist of

Men at Work went from being an obscure Australian band to the top of the charts with their 1982 debut album *Business as Usual*.

1982. Their debut album was so successful that Columbia held the release of their follow-up album, *Cargo*, for almost a year so that it would not cut into sales of the first album. When it was finally released in April 1983, *Cargo* debuted at number thirty, while *Business as Usual* was still in the top five. Less than a month later, Men at Work had two albums in the top ten.

Cargo was as successful as *Business as Usual*, going double platinum with its hit singles "Overkill," "It's a Mistake," and "Dr. Heckyll and Mr. Jive." Success, however, did not bode well for the band. As they began work on their third album, *Two Hearts*, the band started fighting among themselves over management and songwriting. Hay, Ham, and Strykert kicked Speiser and Rees out of the band in 1984. Hay and Ham also decided to produce the new album themselves instead of relying on Peter Mclan, who had produced the first two. Strykert then grew weary of the infighting and left the band before *Two Hearts* was released in 1985. The album proved to be a huge disappointment, and the remaining band members dissolved their partnership a few months later.

German pop star known simply as Nena scored her only hit with "99 Luft Balloons." Two versions of the video aired on MTV, one in English and one in German. The British band After the Fire scored a hit with "Der Kommisar" after they had already broken up and despite record company worries about their Christian leanings. In 1982, Toni Basil, a choreographer and sometime actress who had worked on the Monkees' 1969 cult movie, *Head*, and who had advised the likes of David Bowie, Tina Turner, and Talking Heads on their stage moves, decided to make a record and video of her own and scored a number one hit with "Mickey." *Rolling Stone* described the song as "cheerleader vocals and a backing track that merges eighties funk with sixties garage rock."

If there was one glaring omission from the MTV rotation, however, it was African American artists. In the December 1983 issue of *Rolling Stone*, Steven Levy wrote, "Of the over 750 videos shown on MTV during the channel's first eighteen months, fewer than two dozen featured black artists, even including such racially mixed bands as the English Beat." As MTV became more and more popular, a growing number of journalists and black artists began levying charges of racism. Rick James couldn't get MTV to air his clips for "Super Freak" and "Give It to Me Baby" despite the fact that his album *Street Songs* had sold more than 3 million copies in 1982. After being rejected, a justifiably bitter James took every opportunity he could to slam MTV in the press as a racist network. Executive vice president and chief operating officer Robert Puttman defended MTV's practices by saying

Above: **Michael Jackson broke the "color barrier" of MTV in the early 1980s and has gone on to be one of the most successful, if not eccentric, MTV stars.** Opposite: **Cheerleader chic—choreographer, actress, performance artist Toni Basil in the video for "Mickey."**

that from its inception the channel had positioned itself as a rock and roll station, and that they did air videos by black artists who fit the definition of rock and roll—a curious claim when many of the new pop bands were playing music that was actually closer in sound and attitude to disco than it was to rock and roll.

It was Michael Jackson who was credited with finally breaking the "MTV color barrier" with his videos for "Billie Jean," "Beat It," and "Thriller," three videos that MTV initially hedged on because "they weren't rock and roll." Only after Jackson became a colossal superstar and Columbia Records made some not-so-subtle prods did MTV agree to air the clips. A few short years later, MTV would dedicate an entire week of programming to Michael Jackson, who was by then their biggest star.

Technopop

Ever since Robert Moog unveiled his mini-Moog synthesizer in 1970, synthesized sounds and electronic keyboards have played a major role in popular music. For the first time, virtually any band could afford to add this suitcase-size, virtually unlimited collection of warbling, searing, gurgling, and humming sounds to their repertoire. Brian Eno was one of the first musicians to thoroughly explore the uses of the synthesizer in rock and roll in the early 1970s in his work with Roxy Music and David Bowie—two acts who inspired many of the new wave pop bands, especially the new romantics.

In 1974, the German group Kraftwerk released the first all-electronic pop single, "Autobahn," an edited version of a twenty-two-minute track about a monotonous journey along the famous superhighway. This unusual single rose all the way to number five on the U.S. charts. Their 1977 follow-up singles "Trans-Europe Express" and "Showroom Dummies" both became hits in discos in the United States and England. The band was so enamored of synthesizers, sequencers, and programming that they once talked about touring the United States using only their hardware and

Above: **David Bowie was an important influence on new wave music, especially on the new romantics (see chapter two).** Opposite: **Brian Eno pioneered the use of the synthesizer in rock music in his work with Roxy Music and David Bowie.**

Above: Ultrarox was one of the first post-punk bands to completely do away with guitars in favor of the synthesizer. Opposite: When Midge Ure joined Ultravox in 1980 to replace founder John Foxx, the band really took off.

electronic dummies; the musicians themselves would stay at home. Luckily for their fans, the "non-tour" never materialized. Instead, the "Showroom Dummies" completed the tour dressed as mannequins. Kraftwerk is universally cited as the major influence of synth-oriented bands of the 1980s.

Ultravox was one such band that was heavily influenced by the German electronic quartet. One of the first post-punk bands to completely do away with guitars in favor of synthesizers, Ultravox paved the way for the technopop bands that would hit it big during the MTV era. After vocalist Midge Ure (formerly with ex–Sex Pistol Glen Matlock's Rich Kids) replaced original singer and founder John Foxx in 1980, Ultravox landed seven top 10 U.K. albums and five top 20 singles, but never really broke into the United States (the George Martin–produced *Quartet* peaked at number sixty-one for their highest American charting).

The first technopop star to make an impact in both the United Kingdom and the United States was a balding, diminutive synthesizer enthusiast named Gary Numan (born Gary Webb). Originally a guitar player and singer, Numan started as the front man for an angry punk band called Tubeway Army that released two singles, "That's Not It" and "Bombers." But when the band went into the studio to cut its first album, Numan discovered the synthesizer and put down his guitar forever. Numan's band rebelled against the synth-conversion and left him to record his album with only the aid of his bass player, Paul Gardiner (Numan had to recruit his uncle Jess to play drums). Numan's first two albums, *Tubeway Army* and *Replicas*, were credited to Gary Numan and the Tubeway Army anyway. *Replicas* yielded the British number-one hit "Are 'Friends' Electric?" Numan's big U.S. hit came from his third album, a solo release called *The Pleasure Principle*. From this album, the dance-rock hit "Cars" rushed to the top of the U.K. charts and peaked in the U.S. at number nine. To support the record, Numan toured the United States with an elaborate show that featured robots, fluorescent tubes, and a pyramid-shaped stage. All of the futuristic packaging and artificial sounds, however, could not hide the fact that Numan's music was very simplistic and not very interesting. By 1981, the technopop pioneer retired from the music business to become a professional pilot.

Aside from the futuristic allure of the synthesizer, one aspect of technopop (and eighties new pop in general) was its danceability. Prior to 1983, New Order, made up of the surviving members of Joy Division after the death of lead singer Ian Curtis, was not particularly known for

Opposite: **After helping to bring synth-pop to the forefront of the 1980s musical landscape, Gary Numan became a professional pilot in 1981 and flew around the world.** Below: **After Joy Division lead singer Ian Curtis killed himself in 1980, the remaining members of the band (with the addition of keyboardist Gillian Gilbert [left]) reformed as New Order.**

its dance beat. Like Joy Division, New Order played moody music that exerted a dark vision popular among fans of goth (see page 56) and industrial. A band dedicated mostly to recorded music, New Order's live shows were often very low-key, with the band seemingly more concerned about the after-show party than the performance. During a show in 1983, Stephen Morris turned on his drum machine while the band walked offstage in the hopes of avoiding an encore. Gillian Gilbert threw a sequencer line to the mix to add a little more interest, and when Peter Hook added a programmed bass line, the band had the beginnings of a new song.

Legend has it that New Order later took the programs into the studio, dropped some acid, and pieced things together into an eight-minute song. The result, "Blue Monday," was pressed into a twelve-inch single, was distributed to clubs, and soon replaced Olivia Newton-John's "Physical" as the hot new dance track. "Blue Monday" sold more than 3 million copies worldwide and proved to be New Order's biggest hit. More importantly, it forged a link between the alternative, post-punk music scene and the mainstream dance world, essentially making it cool to dance again.

Aside from a few powerpop and new wave bands, most of the artists that made up the new pop were very dependent on the synthesizer and the electronic keyboard for their sound. Some bands, such as Orchestral Manoeuvers in the Dark (OMD), Depeche Mode, Spandau Ballet, Soft Cell, and A Flock of Seagulls, used the keyboard as the cornerstone of their music. Others, such as Modern English, used the keyboard to complement their pop sensibilities—or psychedelic leanings, as in the case of the Psychedelic Furs. New wave's fascination with electronic music is ironic in that most of the bands claimed a direct descent from the Sex Pistols and the punk movement of the mid-seventies. The punks, for the most part, loathed the synthesizer and made little if any use of the keyboard in general. In fact, most of what is characteristic about new pop goes against just about everything that punk stood for. The music wasn't rebellious—it embraced the star system—and the majority of bands who played it were in it for the fame and money as much as their love of music.

Below: **A meandering synthesizer, jangling guitars, and a driving beat were key ingredients to Modern English's 1983 hit "I Melt with You."** Opposite: **Kraftwerk fans Paul Humphrey and Andy McCluskey of Orchestral Manoeuvres in the Dark (OMD) originally performed live backed by a four-track tape machine they called "Winston." They later added a live rhythm section.**

Goth

The darker side of the 1980s sound, goth was a form of post-punk music that eschewed the feel-good silliness of the new pop in favor of a darker vision and dirge-like music. Bands such as Siouxsie and the Banshees, the Cure, Echo and the Bunnymen, and Bauhaus held on to some of the punk rock pessimism in their music while maintaining the reliance on fashion, synthesized music, and danceability that helped define other forms of eighties music. Boy George would prance around the stage wearing a long colorful frock, but Robert Smith of the Cure would stalk about looking like an underfed vampire with jet black hair and pale skin and singing with a diffident, quavering voice. With its brooding lyrics and gloomy minor-key melodies, goth is perhaps the darkest of the postpunk musical styles of the early 1980s. It is epitomized by lots of black—black velvet, black makeup, black hair—to set off the paleness of pancake white skin. In the early 1980s, the goth scene was centered around the Batcave in London and such bands as Alien Sex Fiend, Sisters of Mercy, Sex Gang Children, and the American contributors, Christian Death and the Cramps. One of the first signature tunes of goth was the Bauhaus hit "Bela

Left: The grand dame of goth, Siouxise Sioux of Siouxsie and the Banshees. Opposite: The early Cure with Robert Smith (left), Matthew Hartley (middle), and Robert Tolhurst (right).

Lugosi's Dead," a ten-minute epic where the cadaverously pale Peter Murphy sings about bats and the walking dead. As the trend hit its peak, bands like Nick Cave and the Birthday put on elaborate stage shows to accompany their psychedelic dirge and ranting vocals.

Goth got its name when the British press started describing the music of Siouxsie and the Banshees as "English Gothic." Siouxsie Sioux (born Susan Dallion) was a ubiquitous punk rock fan and a member of the Bromley Contingent, a dedicated group of Sex Pistols fans (one other member of the Bromley Contingent was Sid Vicious, who would later join the Sex Pistols himself).

Embracing the punk creed that everyone can and should start a band, Siouxsie formed the Banshees in 1976 with Steve Severin on bass, Marco Pirroni (who would later join Adam and the Ants) on guitar, and Sid Vicious on drums. The Banshees' first performance, at the 1976 100 Club Punk Festival, consisted of a twenty-minute version of "The Lord's Prayer," which included parts of "Twist & Shout," "Rebel Rebel," and "Knockin' on Heaven's Door." Over the next few years, the Banshees changed personnel, added Cure leader Robert Smith, got their musical act together, and gradually drifted away from punk and toward the gloomy dark music that would be known as goth. With the change in music came a change in Siouxsie's wardrobe—from safety pins and see-through blouses to blood red velvet that set off her jet black hair.

Robert Smith (who was once described as the "guru of gloom") left the Banshees in 1984 to devote himself full-time to the Cure. Siouxsie Sioux persisted, however, and remains the elder states-woman of goth. The band broke up in 1996.

Conclusion

By the mid to late 1980s, many of the bands written about here either no longer existed or were well past their prime. Boy George, the poster boy for the eighties' new pop, had lost his band, cut his hair, and was battling heroin addiction. Men at Work and A Flock of Seagulls, two of the original "MTV bands," had drifted into obscurity after being unable to replicate their initial successes. Duran Duran still plugged along, but an increasingly cynical public grew tired of their pseudo-sophisticated, hair-blown image.

The musical landscape of the early 1980s had been marked by overnight successes and synth-driven dance-pop. In the music industry's search for the next big thing, it seemed as if any band with big hair, an unusual name, and a good video or two had a shot at instant stardom, no matter how fleeting that fame might be.

Taken as a whole, the bands that made up the new pop sound of the 1980s helped revitalize the music industry and change the direction and attitude of popular music, but by the end of the 1980s, popular music was no longer ruled by the British club bands. American superstars Michael Jackson, Bruce Springsteen, Prince, Madonna, and a revamped Tina Turner entered the MTV mix and enjoyed record sales

Above: by the mid 1980s, American superstars like Madonna ruled the MTV air waves and the British club bands of the early 1980s were quickly becoming a memory. Opposite: In the mid 1980s, ABC dropped their preening, well-coifed image for a more eclectic one.

and stardom that far surpassed even that of the most popular new pop bands. The high-glam technopop of Human League and ABC was replaced by the glam-metal of Def Leppard, Van Halen, Mötley Crüe, and Twisted Sister. After a few short years enjoying the MTV limelight, the new pop bands of the early 1980s were no longer "the next big thing."

Recommended Listening

ABC, *Lexicon of Love*, Polygram, 1982

Adam Ant, *Antics in the Forbidden Zone*, Sony, 1990

Bow Wow Wow, *I Want Candy*, BMG/RCA, 1982

Culture Club, *Colour By Numbers*, Virgin, 1983

Cure, *Boys Don't Cry*, Elektra, 1980

Duran Duran, *Decade: Greatest Hits*, Capitol, 1989

Go-Go's, *Beauty and the Beat*, I.R.S., 1981

Human League, *Greatest Hits*, A&M, 1988

Malcolm McLaren, *Fans*, PolyGram, 1984

Men at Work, *Business as Usual*, Sony, 1981

Psychedelic Furs, *Psychedelic Furs*, Sony, 1980

Siouxsie and the Banshees, *Twice Upon a Time*, Geffen, 1992

Thompson Twins, *Into the Gap*, Arista, 1984

Ultravox, *Vienna*, Chrysalis, 1981

Further Reading

Clarke, Donald, ed. *The Penguin Encyclopedia of Popular Music.* New York: Viking/Penguin, 1989.

Clarke, Donald. *The Rise and Fall of Popular Music.* New York: St. Martin's Press, 1995.

Cross, Alan. *The Alternative Music Almanac.* Chicago: Collector's Guide Publishing, 1995.

Decurtis, Anthony, James Henke, Holly George-Warren, and Jim Miller, eds. *The Rolling Stone Illustrated History of Rock and Roll: The Definitive History of the Most Important Artists & Their Music.* New York: Random House, 1992.

Du Noyer, Paul S. *The Story of Rock'n'Roll.* New York: Macmillan, 1995.

Fornatale, Pete. *The Story of Rock'n'Roll.* New York: William Morrow and Company, 1987.

Friedlander, Paul. *Rock and Roll: A Social History.* Boulder, Co: Westview Press, 1996.

Heylin, Clinton. *From the Velvets to the Voidoids: A Pre-Punk History for a Post-Punk World.* New York, Penguin: 1996.

Marcus, Greil. *Lipstick Traces: A Secret History of the Twentieth Century.* Cambridge, Ma: Harvard University Press, 1989.

McNeil, Legs and Gillian McCain. *Please Kill Me: The Uncensored Oral History of Punk.* New York: Grove/Atlantic, 1996.

Palmer, Robert. *Rock and Roll: An Unruly History.* New York: Harmony, 1995.

Rimmer, Dave. *Like Punk Never Happened: Culture Club and the New Pop.* London: Faber and Faber, 1985.

Romanowski, Patricia, ed. *New Rolling Stone Encyclopedia of Rock and Roll.* New York: Fireside, 1995.

Savage, Jon. *England's Dreaming: Anarchy, Sex Pistol, Punk, Rock and Beyond.* New York: St. Martin's Press, 1993.

Szatmary, David P. *Rockin' in Time: A Social History of Rock and Roll.* New York: Prentice Hall, 1995.

Photography Credits

Front Jacket, Box, Jewel Case and Compact Disc Label Photography (Clock-wise from top): Retna Ltd.: ©Robert Matheu; Retna Ltd.: ©Barry Schultz; everett collection, inc.: ©Tom Sheehan; Retna Ltd.: ©Mark Lebon

everett collection, inc.: p. 36

Photofeatures International: RE-LAY: p. 39, ©Andre Csillag: p. 40

Retna Ltd.: ©Janette Beckman: pp. 30, 35; ©Adrian Boot: pp. 16-17, 34; ©Caroline Coon: pp. 20-21; ©David Corio: p. 9; ©Kevin Cummins: p. 53; ©Michael D'Adamo: p. 47; ©Kevin Davies: p. 28; ©Jill Furmanovsky: pp. 10, 38, 57; ©Gary Gershoff: pp. 26-27, 44-45, 59; ©Donald Greenhaus: p. 11; ©Lisa Haun: p. 54; ©Ian Hooton: p. 51; ©Mark Lebon: p. 32; ©Robert Matheu: p. 2; ©Neil Matthews: p. 58; ©Walter McBride: p. 22; ©Tony Mottram: p. 52; ©Jonathan Postal: p. 6; ©Michael Putland: pp. 29, 49, 56; ©Barry Schultz: p. 23; ©Peter Simon: p. 19; ©Stevenson: p. 48; ©Joe Stevenson: pp. 43, ghosted back-grounds; ©Ray Stevenson: pp. 14-15, 16, 18; ©Ann Summa: p. 55; ©Chris Walter: p. 42; ©Ron Wolfson: p. 46; Redferns: ©Ian Dickson: p. 12

Rex USA LTD.: pp. 12-13; RDR Productions: pp. 8, 31, ©Allan Ballard: pp. 21 top, 25

Courtesy of **Showtime Music Archives**, Toronto: pp. 24, 50-51

Index